A live in 5

Raw Gourmet Meals in Five Minutes!

by
Angela Elliott

Book Publishing Company
Summertown, Tennessee

Cover design: Warren Jefferson
Interior design: Gwynelle Dismukes
Photography: Warren Jefferson
Food styling: Barbara Jefferson, Melina Bloomfield

Published in the United States by
Book Publishing Company
P.O. Box 99, Summertown, TN 38483
1-888-260-8458   www.bookpubco.com

Printed in Canada.

ISBN 978-1-57067-202-6

12 11 10 09 08 07   6 5 4 3 2

Elliott, Angela J.
  Alive in five : raw gourmet meals in five minutes/by Angela Elliott.
    p. cm.
  Includes bibliographical references and index.
  ISBN 978-1-57067-202-6 (alk. paper)
  1. Cookery (Natural foods) 2. Raw foods. 3. Quick and easy cookery. I. Title.
  TX741.E47 2007
  641.5'63--dc22   2006036526

Book Publishing Co. is a member of Green Press Initiative. We chose to print this title on paper with postconsumer recycled content, processed without chlorine, which prevented the following waste of natural resources:

BOOK
PUBLISHING
COMPANY

44 trees
2,079 pounds of solid waste
16,188 gallons of water
3,900 pounds of greenhouse gases
31 million BTUs of energy

green press
INITIATIVE

For more information, visit <www.greenpressinitiative.org>. Savings calculations thanks to the Environmental Defense Paper Calculator, <www.papercalculator.org>.

Contents

$\mathcal{F}$oreword

In this neat book, *Alive in Five*, Angela Elliott demonstrates how raw food meals can be healthful, fun, and easy. With a sparkle and a smile, she adds a delightful melody to her flavorful, nutrient-packed, gourmet raw cuisine, making excellent nutrition accessible to even first-timers.

The recipes are easy to follow and quick to prepare. Angela is truly a wizard in the kitchen and definitely has the rare gift to excite every aspect of your taste buds.

Angela is not only a wonderful chef, she is also a compassionate and loving person. In this book she shares with you her journey to health and how she overcame many obstacles she faced along the way. From my own personal experience of knowing Angela for many years, I know she loves to share her vast knowledge with all who need her assistance and guidance.

It is because of the overwhelming response to her food that she passionately chose to write this book. Her hope is to empower every reader to make choices with high integrity while enjoying delicious food.

Angela understands that illness is a teacher, and if we listen to its message, it can direct us back to the smooth, wide-open freeway of health, opportunity, and limitless possibility. She also understands that mineral-rich, enzyme-active plant foods play a major role in healing and spiritual growth.

The intimate connection between fresh food and health is continuing to be the most influential factor in the minds and hearts of those interested in longevity, spirituality, and rejuvenation. In this context, I regard Angela's book as an important contribution to this growing movement.

—*David Wolfe*

Author of *The Sunfood Diet Success System*, *Eating for Beauty*, and *Naked Chocolate*. Founder of www.rawfood.com and director of the nonprofit Fruit Tree Planting Foundation, www.fruittreefoundation.org.

Preface

I'm not going to go into a long list of details on why you should eat raw food. Everyone knows the importance of adding fruits and vegetables to their diet. It's discussed in books and magazines and on television and radio programs. In fact, it's advice that can be found just about anywhere.

Alive in Five isn't a book about dogma; it's about having fun in the kitchen and getting healthy doing it. *Alive in Five* is for people who want to add some spice to their lives, improve their health, prepare foods in fresh, exciting ways, and awaken their taste buds, all at the same time.

In *Alive in Five* you will discover how easy it is to prepare living cuisine in about five minutes, with very little equipment and easy-to-find ingredients. You can choose to use only organic ingredients or not, sprout or not sprout, soak or not soak. I provide the guidelines, but the choices are up to you. You can let your imagination lift you wherever you want to go. With raw food, there are no limits!

Anyone can prepare gourmet raw cuisine. From prep to cleanup, it's easy! Just think, you can make an exciting gourmet meal for your friends and family in only about five minutes, clean up the kitchen in under ten minutes, and have time to actually sit and enjoy your guests. Now that's impressive!

Are you concerned that you don't have enough space or the right equipment? Cast away your worries! Even the tiniest kitchen will do; and since most of the recipes just require a blender to whip up these gourmet delicacies, you won't be spending your hard-earned money on unnecessary kitchen gadgets.

It's pleasurable to eat raw food. *Alive in Five* cuisine will leave you pleasantly energized, elated, and satisfied, and I know you'll be back for more.

What's all the fuss about raw food anyway? Raw food restaurants, cafés, and mail order companies are springing up all over. Hollywood stars, athletes, and everyday people like you and me are going raw and loving it—and we're sporting great figures to boot.

It seems that raw food may be here to stay. Did you know that the first raw food restaurant opened in Los Angeles back in 1917? It was called The Eutrophean, and was so popular that the owners had to open three of them. These restaurants lasted for 25 years, until World War II.

Alive in Five proves that raw food is more than a boring plate of lettuce, celery, and carrots. In fact, with *Alive in Five* your meals will never be boring again. The recipes in this book are designed to spark your imagination, so you can create your own new recipes from my original ones.

Imagine the pleasures of mouthwatering spinach pie, lasagne, spaghetti marinara, stuffed mushrooms, broccoli in cheese sauce, apple pie, decadent whipped cream and strawberries, or a chocolate shake. It's easy to see how a little creativity can make raw food exciting. *Alive in Five* cuisine has its own personality—it's sassy and playful. You'll soon find that the joy of preparing and eating this food is contagious. Before long, all your friends and family will be joining you!

In time, you may find that you prefer raw food to cooked food. Some people naturally gravitate toward an all-raw diet, while others like having a mix of cooked and raw food. It doesn't matter which you prefer; experts agree that eating more vegetables and fruits will make us all healthier. *Alive in Five* is the perfect book to help you achieve just that.

—*Chef Angela*

Acknowledgments

This book is dedicated to my mother, for helping me in more ways than I can count and for being the best friend any gal could ever have. Mom, thank you. I would also like to thank my son, Ian, and my husband, Mike, for believing in me and supporting me 100 percent. Thanks to all my wonderful friends who helped me with this book: Richard Chisholm, David Wolfe, Michael Pelkey, and Thor. My deepest gratitude to Jo Stepaniak—the greatest editor in the world. Her wonderful artistry permeates this book! Thanks to my entire family and every one of my friends. My life is profoundly richer because of all of you!

My Story

I began my journey with raw food after two near-death experiences and a lifelong battle with chronic pain. Always searching for a cure, I tried virtually every holistic and allopathic approach available. Many years ago, I met two wonderful and inspirational people. They were full of life and beamed with good health. They said their "secret" was raw food, and they suggested that I try it. Because I wanted the same glow of health that they had, I decided to give raw food a chance. At first I wasn't too keen on it, but I couldn't ignore the wonderful way I was beginning to feel. I felt alive, completely energized, and happy. I started looking more fit and beautiful, too. Friends and relatives would tell me, "You are illuminated, Angela!" I was sold! This way of eating has completely transformed me and helped me realize how extraordinary and precious life truly is. I feel a deeper connection to my inner being and to all life on this planet. It is my sincere wish that you, too, will be transformed.

Why "Alive in Five"?

My mother is an extraordinary gourmet French chef. When I was growing up, I used to help her in the kitchen making fresh whipped cream. With big eyes filled with wonder, I would watch her prepare all kinds of amazing delicacies. As if by magic, the whole room would transform into a heavenly masterpiece of exquisite gourmet food. She lived to prepare food for large crowds. Secretly, I wanted to follow in her footsteps and be the gal that everyone thought was a food magician.

What I have found over the years is that I am way too busy to spend all that time in the kitchen. My skill as a gourmet chef has enabled me to make food very quickly yet elegantly. The idea for *Alive in Five* came to me in a dream—a dream so fantastic I had to share it with you!

After tasting my food, many people ask for my help. They are frustrated because, no matter how hard they try, they can't make the complicated, multi-ingredient dishes that are in so many raw food books nowadays. The main reason for their frustration is the time involved in preparing these gourmet dishes. In addition, most raw food books require many different kinds of equipment to make a single recipe. That can be both intimidating and expensive. The only equipment that is essential for making a delicious raw meal is a blender and sometimes a food processor. Almost all the gourmet meals I prepare for my clients are made using a high-speed blender; the remaining food I chop by hand. Believe it or not, chopping by hand, once you become proficient at it, is a relatively fast way of preparing raw dishes. The best blender on the market is the Vita-Mix, because it can handle just about anything you put into it.

My mother is my inspiration for writing this book because she, like so many people I have met, wants to eat healthful, gourmet food, but she lives in a remote area where it is difficult to find anything organic. This book is dedicated to the people who have the fewest resources but try their hardest to become healthy and make their lives more pleasurable. After years of personal experience, I have come to believe that organic food is best for our health and the environment and should be used whenever possible. Unfortunately, not everyone has access to it. If there are farmers in your area, make friends with them. Farmers' markets are a great resource, and if there is one in your area, I encourage you to check it out. Farmers' markets offer everything from fresh herbs and heirloom tomatoes to live plants to start your own garden.

Soon you will be embarking on a blissful culinary journey right in your very own kitchen. Enjoy!

Why Raw Food?

When you eat high-quality raw food, you give your body the fuel it needs to heal and prevent disease. Raw food will give you abundant energy; it will also help you look and feel your best. A raw food diet consists of raw fruits, nuts, seeds, and vegetables. These foods are rich in powerful enzymes, which aid the body in healing. The nutrients in raw food are well assimilated because the food is eaten in its natural, unadulterated state.

Here are some of the many advantages to a raw food diet:
• Lose weight easily and keep it off.
• Look more radiant and beautiful.
• Create optimum health.
• Think more clearly.
• Awaken and renew your spirit.
• Arouse your creative juices.
• Reconnect with your higher self.
• Become more vibrant and passionate.
• Dispel grumpiness, moodiness, and depression.
• Detoxify all areas of your life.
• Sustain the planet by composting fruit and vegetable wastes.
• Stay safe in the kitchen (you can't get burned if you don't cook!).
• Plan meals in minutes.
• Prepare food quickly and easily.
• Clean up the kitchen effortlessly (there are no stuck-on foods or greasy dishes to wash!).
• Have boundless energy.

The Raw Food Pantry

The following pantry staples will allow you to make all the recipes in this book. Most of these ingredients can be found at any well-stocked natural food store. Fresh organic produce is available at some supermarkets, most natural food stores, and many farmers' markets. Any hard-to-find or specialty items may be ordered from the suppliers on page 122.

Agave nectar, raw: This light syrup is the distilled juice of the agave cactus. It is a naturally low-glycemic sweetener.

Almonds, raw: Of all the nuts, almonds are the most beneficial. They easily sprout after soaking, making them highly digestible. Soak almonds for 12–24 hours to optimize their digestibility.

Almond milk: Almond milk is a nondairy beverage made from sprouted almonds that are blended with water.

Almond pulp: This is the moist, nutritious residue that remains after making and straining almond milk. It can be used to make raw desserts, pâtés, and cereals.

Black pepper: Use only freshly milled black pepper.

Cacao beans and nibs, raw: Cacao beans are the seeds of the cacao fruit. They taste like bitter baking chocolate. Nibs are cacao beans that have been chopped into pieces.

Carob powder, raw: Carob comes from the fruit of an evergreen tree native to the Mediterranean region. The tree's large, long, bean-like pods are picked, dried, and ground into a fine powder that looks very similar to cocoa powder.

Cashews, raw: Truly raw cashews have not been heat treated.

Cayenne: This ground red pepper has amazing health benefits. It is excellent for circulation and heart health, and it gives recipes a nice little kick.

Coconuts, young: Contained in freshly picked coconuts is a delicately sweet juice, which, in Asia, is believed to be the best remedy to quench thirst, especially during hot and humid summers. Apart from the delicious juice, young coconuts provide us with their juicy, sweet white meat. Look for young coconuts at Asian markets and natural food stores.

Coconut butter, raw: Coconut butter, also known as coconut oil, is one of the few healthful saturated fats. Coconut butter adds a creamy texture to recipes.

Cremini mushrooms: Creminis are baby portobello mushrooms. They are very nutritious and taste great raw.

Dates, honey: Honey dates are creamy and soft and are the best choice for recipes.

Flaxseeds: Always buy flaxseeds whole rather than ground, because the delicate oil in powdered flaxseeds can go rancid fairly quickly. Flaxseeds are rich in essential omega-3 fatty acids.

Goji berries: Perhaps the most nutritionally rich food on the planet, goji berries contain an amazing number of amino acids, trace minerals, and carotenoids, and have a greater concentration of vitamin C than almost any other food. They have been traditionally regarded as a food to promote longevity, immune system function, and strength. Goji berries are about the size of a raisin and taste like a cross between a cranberry and a cherry.

Hempseeds and hempseed oil, raw: Hempseeds are the world's most nutritious seeds. They are a rich source of omega-3 fatty acids, GLA, vitamin E, iron, and protein. Hempseed oil has nearly the same benefits as the seeds and imparts a lovely nutty flavor to recipes.

Himalayan salt: Himalayan salt is the cleanest, purest, and most complete salt available. It contains over 80 elements and trace minerals.

Macadamia nuts, raw: Macadamia nuts are a powerhouse of nutrients. Macadamia nuts are used to make fantastic creamy raw sauces and whipped cream.

Miso, unpasteurized: Miso is a salty, fermented Japanese seasoning paste that is traditionally made from soybeans and sometimes grain. It is aged from several months to several years. Although not raw, miso is a wonderful source of live enzymes and friendly bacteria that aid digestion. Look for it in the refrigerated section of your natural food store.

Nama Shoyu: This unique brand of soy sauce is aged like miso. Although it is not raw, it contains healthful live enzymes and other beneficial organisms. It imparts a lovely soy sauce flavor with significantly lower sodium.

Nutritional yeast: Nutritional yeast is a cheesy-tasting, nutrient-rich seasoning that comes in powder or flakes. It is vegan but not raw. Look for nutritional yeast in the bulk section of your natural food store or buy it from the suppliers listed on page 122.

Olives, organic raw: The best raw olives are cured in Himalayan salt, filtered water, spices, and hot peppers. They are beautiful, mineral rich, and very tasty in raw recipes.

Olive oil, cold-pressed extra-virgin: Olive oil is cold-pressed from olives. As with fine wine, the climate and region of origin determine the taste. The best olive oils are smooth, vibrant, and bold.

Pine nuts, raw: Also called pignolis or piñons, pine nuts come from the pinecone of the piñon tree.

Probiotic powder: This supplement powder provides friendly bacteria for the intestinal tract. It is essential for making my vegan yogurts. I recommend New Chapter brand.

Produce: Local stores that sell organic fruits and vegetables and farmers' markets are the best sources.

Pumpkin seeds, raw: Pumpkin seeds are beneficial for ridding the body of parasites and similar unwanted "guests." They are high in zinc and other important nutrients, and are delicious in recipes.

Raisins: Delicious sun-dried grapes are marvelous in raw cereals.

Sea vegetables, raw: The sea vegetable used in my recipes is raw nori.

Spices and seasoning blends: Blends are typically combinations of dried herbs and spices. The best ones do not contain salt.

Sun-dried tomatoes: Use only unsulfured tomatoes that have been sun-dried, not oven-baked at high temperatures.

Tahini, raw: Tahini is a smooth spread made from finely ground sesame seeds.

Vanilla beans: Vanilla beans come from Madagascar. They are very expensive, but the flavor is well worth the cost.

Vanilla flavor: This is a pure glycerite that only contains the essence of vanilla. It contains no sugars, alcohol, or artificial flavorings.

Walnuts, raw: Walnuts are highly nutritious and comparatively inexpensive. They are used in many of my recipes.

Essential Equipment

Bamboo sushi mat: A sushi mat makes rolling raw vegan sushi easy and fun. They are available at most Asian stores.

Coffee grinder: An electric coffee grinder is used to grind whole spices and seeds. Any model will do. Coffee grinders are available at most kitchen and discount stores.

Food processor: Food processors make easy work of chopping or mincing ingredients. The brands I recommend are Cuisinart and Black and Decker Power Pro II.

Ice cream maker: I recommend the Cuisinart brand Frozen Yogurt, Sorbet, and Ice Cream Maker, available at most kitchen specialty stores.

Knives: Essential knives for preparing raw food include a chef's knife, paring knife, and a cleaver for opening young coconuts. These can be found at specialty kitchen stores. Always keep your knives sharpened and well cared for.

Spiral slicer: This tool is so much fun! It quickly and easily creates noodle shapes from vegetables. Spiral slicers are available from the suppliers listed on page 122.

Strainer: I recommend OXO brand. It is available at most kitchenware and discount stores.

Vita-Mix: The Vita-Mix is a heavy-duty blender that can handle practically anything you put into it. My Vita-Mix is sometimes used as often as 10 times a day. I wouldn't own any other brand. It is available from www.vitamix.com or the suppliers listed on page 122.

Helpful Tips

- Soaking nuts makes them more digestible. It also makes them creamier when used in recipes. Simply place raw nuts or seeds in a bowl and add enough filtered water to cover them. Let nuts soak for 12–24 hours and seeds for 3 hours, then drain.

- If soaked nuts or seeds are needed quickly for a recipe, soak them for just 1 hour and drain.

- In order to be able to prepare recipes on a moment's notice, always keep soaked nuts and seeds on hand. Stored in a covered container in the refrigerator, they will keep for up to three days.

- When making nut milk, be sure to use a fine mesh strainer to catch all the pulp. A very fine strainer will ensure that your milk is smooth and creamy.

- Save the pulp from Almond Milk (page 31) to use in Cinnamon Apple Cereal (page 36) or Going Nuts Pâté Rolls (page 43).

- Save the pulp from Pecan Milk (page 34) to make Happy Porridge (page 39).

- Save the pulp from Luscious Walnut Milk (page 111) to make Decadent Whipped Cream and Strawberries (page 110) or Celestial Fettuccine Alfredo (page 80).

- To make raw meals on short notice, always have something soaking, marinating, and/or ripening.

- Keeping a well-stocked kitchen is essential for making gourmet meals in under five minutes.

- Keep grated carrots on hand for use in a variety of recipes. Stored in a covered container in the refrigerator, grated carrots will keep for up to two days.

- Sliced zucchinis can be marinated in olive oil and salt and kept in the refrigerator for two days before using in any of the pasta recipes in this book.

A Guide to Fruits

Apples contain pectin, a soluble fiber that is highly effective in lowering cholesterol. Apples stimulate the body's digestive secretions and are beneficial for constipation and a sluggish liver.

Apricots are high in vitamin A and several minerals, including iron. They cleanse impurities from the blood and help overcome anemia, high-acid conditions, and sluggish digestion. Apricots have been known to ease inflammation of the bronchial tubes.

Avocados, rich in essential fatty acids, are excellent for the heart, brain, and skin.

Bananas are rich in potassium and provide quick yet sustained energy, making them the perfect fruit for athletes. They have been known to heal diarrhea, colitis, and ulcers, and even help with constipation.

Blueberries are amazing blood cleansers and help ease inflammation. Anemia, constipation, diarrhea, and menstrual disorders can all be helped by the regular addition of blueberries to the diet.

Cantaloupe is rich in minerals, including potassium, and vitamins A and C. Cantaloupe can help heal constipation, stiff joints, blood disorders, and obesity.

Cherries are rich in magnesium and iron. They are a wonderful cleanser for the kidneys, liver, and urinary system. Cherries are excellent for arthritis, high blood pressure, and anemia.

Cranberries are helpful to the kidneys and bladder because their natural acidity creates an environment in which bacteria cannot thrive. Cranberries have been used for centuries to clarify the complexion.

Dates are an energy-giving source of dietary fiber, potassium, and iron.

Grapes, both purple and green, provide easily assimilated natural sugars. Not only do grapes provide quick energy, they are a potent cleanser of the liver and kidneys.

Kiwis are higher in vitamin C than most other fruits.

Lemons are a natural antiseptic, making them a powerful internal cleanser for the entire body.

Mangoes help strengthen poor digestion and overcome acidity in the body. They are excellent for calming inflamed kidneys. Mangoes are rich in beta-carotene.

Oranges help alleviate high blood pressure, lung problems, and conditions related to vitamin C deficiency. Oranges are alkalizing to the body.

Papayas are rich in the enzyme papain, which helps correct problems in the digestive system. Both papaya flesh and juice remove cellular waste and mucus in the colon and stomach. Papayas contain a large quantity of alkaline minerals, especially calcium, vitamin A (which is unusual in fruit), and a high concentration of collagen-healing vitamin C.

Peaches improve the color and health of the complexion and skin. Their high vitamin and mineral content makes them valuable in the treatment of anemia, sluggish digestion, and high-acid conditions in the blood.

Plums are great energizers and cleansers of the intestinal tract. Their mild laxative properties give them the ability to relieve gas and hemorrhoids.

Raspberries have the ability to heal obesity, high blood pressure, and constipation. Raspberries are an excellent source of vitamins C and A.

Strawberries rid the bloodstream, liver, and intestines of toxins. They can also benefit stiff joints and rid the body of excess catarrh.

For more information on these and other fruits and vegetables, please consult *Eating for Beauty* by David Wolfe.

Storing Fruits and Vegetables

Apples and pears are best stored in a bowl on the table, not hidden in a refrigerator where they tend to lose their crispness.

Apricots and peaches are best stored in a bowl and eaten within the first day or two after purchasing.

Avocados should be stored in the refrigerator if ripe or nearly ripe; if unripe, store them in a bowl at room temperature until they reach the desired ripeness.

Bananas will keep well in a fruit bowl until you are ready to use them. The riper they are, the sweeter they are.

Berries should be refrigerated. Do not wash berries until just before using them or they will spoil.

Cantaloupes and honeydews are best stored on the counter until you are ready to eat them.

Carrots are best stored in the refrigerator.

Cherries should be stored in a bag in the fruit drawer of your refrigerator.

Young coconuts taste best when they are used right away, but they will keep for about 10 days in the refrigerator.

Cranberries should be kept in the refrigerator until you are ready to use them.

Dates should be stored whole and unpitted in a sealed container in a cool, dry place until you are ready to use them.

Fresh figs should be refrigerated if they are not eaten immediately.

Grapes are best stored in a colander in the refrigerator.

Grapefruits keep well without refrigeration.

Kiwis keep best in the refrigerator.

Lemons and limes store well at room temperature, but if it is particularly hot where you live, you should refrigerate them for longer storage.

Mangoes ripen well when sitting in a fruit bowl at room temperature.

Nectarines ripen well in a fruit bowl at room temperature, but keep an eye on them to make sure they do not rot before you get the chance to eat them.

Oranges and tangerines store well in the refrigerator.

Papayas will keep a few days without refrigeration, but once they have ripened they should be eaten right away.

Passion fruit stores well in the refrigerator.

Persimmons ripen at room temperature and are best eaten as soon as they are ripe.

Pineapples are best eaten right away, if ripe.

Plums store well at room temperature and are best eaten immediately after ripening.

Raisins should be kept in a sealed container and stored in a cool, dry place.

Strawberries are best eaten right away.

Watermelons are best eaten right away.

A Menu Plan for One Week

Equipment
blender
chef's knife
cutting board
ice cube tray
measuring cup
orange juice squeezer

Pantry Staples
agave nectar, raw
basil, dried
cashews, raw
cayenne
coconut oil, raw
dates
dill weed, dried
Himalayan salt
Mexican seasoning
Nama Shoyu
nori, raw
olive oil, cold-pressed
    extra-virgin
onion powder
peppercorns, black
probiotic powder
raisins
tarragon, dried
tomatoes, sun-dried
vanilla beans
vanilla flavor

Fresh Produce
apples
avocados
bananas
basil
bell peppers
blueberries
broccoli
carrots
celery
Chinese cabbage
cilantro
coconuts, young
cucumbers
garlic
jalapeño chiles
lemons
lettuce
oranges
salad mix
snow peas
sprouts, mung bean
strawberries
tangerines
tomatoes, Roma
zucchinis

Additional Items
almonds, raw
cherries, frozen organic
corn, frozen organic
ginger, fresh
hemp oil, raw
ice cubes
miso, unpasteurized
pineapple, frozen
sunflower seeds, raw
walnuts, raw

A Menu Plan for One Week

Day 1

Breakfast: Whipped Orange Shake (page 33)

Lunch: The Garden Salad (page 60)

Dinner: Cream of Zucchini Soup (page 62)

Dessert: Life's a Bowl of Cherries Sorbet (page 121)

Day 2

Breakfast: Scrambled "Eggs" (page 38)

Lunch: Crème Tomat (page 67)

Dinner: Zippy "Tuna" Rolls (page 84)

Day 3

Breakfast: Nut Yogurt with Fresh Berries (page 37)

Lunch: Junk Food Salad (page 48)

Dinner: Corn Symphony (page 65)

Day 4

Breakfast: Jazzy Piña Colada Smoothie (page 29)

Lunch: On the Orient (page 49)

Dinner: Hot! Hot! Hot! Aguacate Soup (page 63)

Dessert: Tangerine Dream (page 106)

Day 5

Breakfast: Banana Shake (page 30)

Lunch: Stuffed Peppers (page 89)

Dinner: Fashionable Carrot and Raisin Salad (page 53)

Day 6

Breakfast: Happy Porridge (page 39)

Lunch: Caesar's Delight (page 57)

Dinner: Celestial Fettuccine Alfredo (page 80)

Day 7

Breakfast: Cinnamon Apple Cereal (page 36)

Lunch: Hey, It's Raita! (page 52)

Dinner: Herb-Infused Soup (page 64)

Beverages

Velvety Dessert Milk

Makes 8 cups

This milk is creamy, rich, and naturally sweet.

---

7 cups filtered water
1 cup soaked raw almonds
10 pitted honey dates
$\frac{1}{2}$ vanilla bean
1 teaspoon raw agave nectar
$\frac{1}{8}$ teaspoon Himalayan salt

Combine the water and almonds in a blender, and process until smooth. Strain, and set aside the pulp for another recipe. Rinse out the blender jar and pour the milk back into it. Add the remaining ingredients, and process until very smooth and creamy.

Jazzy Piña Colada Smoothie

Makes 2 servings

This smoothie is an excellent children's drink.

1 young coconut, water and meat
1½ cups frozen pineapple chunks
1 Valencia orange, peeled and seeded
2 orange slices (optional)

Combine the coconut water and meat, pineapple chunks, and Valencia orange in a blender, and process until smooth. Serve in tall glasses garnished with a slice of orange, if desired.

Variation

Banana-Mango Piña Colada Smoothie: Add 1 ripe banana, 1 ripe mango, and a small amount of shredded dried coconut (optional).

Note: This smoothie is a real crowd pleaser. It can easily be doubled or tripled to serve more people.

Lovely Strawberry Smoothie

Makes 5 servings

This creamy smoothie is strawberry heaven.

5 cups Velvety Dessert Milk (page 28)
1 cup (about 5 ounces) fresh strawberries
1 cup (about 8 ounces) frozen pineapple chunks
1 ripe banana

Combine all the ingredients in a blender, and process until smooth.

Banana Shake

Makes 2 servings

This shake is bursting with banana flavor.

1 cup Luscious Walnut Milk (page 111)
2 ripe bananas
4 pitted dates, soaked
1 teaspoon vanilla flavor

Combine all the ingredients in a blender, and process until smooth.

Almond Milk

Makes 6 servings

Almond milk is incredibly versatile. Its subtle flavor makes it ideal for adding to recipes, but it is also delicious on its own.

5 cups filtered water
1 cup soaked raw almonds
3 tablespoons raw agave nectar
$1\frac{1}{2}$ tablespoons vanilla flavor
$\frac{1}{8}$ teaspoon Himalayan salt

Combine the water and almonds in a blender, and process until smooth. Strain, and set aside the pulp for another recipe. Rinse out the blender jar and pour the milk back into it. Add the remaining ingredients, and process until smooth and creamy.

Hempseed Milk

Makes 6 servings

Hempseeds are nourishing and tasty. This milk can be enjoyed as is or added to shakes.

5 cups filtered water

1 cup raw hempseeds

$1/2$ cup raw agave nectar

1 tablespoon vanilla flavor

$1/8$ teaspoon Himalayan salt

Combine all the ingredients in a blender, and process until smooth.

Whipped Orange Shake, page 33
Nut Yogurt with Fresh Berries, page 37

Pecan Milk

Makes 6 servings

This milk reminds me of eggnog, except it's a lot tastier.

5 cups filtered water
1 cup soaked raw pecans
3 tablespoons raw agave nectar
1 1/2 tablespoons vanilla flavor
1/8 teaspoon Himalayan salt

Combine the water and pecans in a blender, and process until smooth. Strain, and set aside the pulp for another recipe. Rinse out the blender jar and pour the milk back into it. Add the remaining ingredients, and process until smooth and creamy.

Whipped Orange Shake

Makes 2 servings   *See photo facing page 32.*

*This is our favorite shake. It reminds me of an Orange
Julius or an Orange Dream Bar. Delicious!*

2 cups freshly squeezed orange juice
1 1/2 cups ice cubes
1 ripe banana

Combine all the ingredients in a blender, and process until smooth.

Cucumber Pizzas, page 42
Going Nuts Pâté Rolls, page 43
Stuffed Mushrooms, page 46

Breakfast

Cinnamon Apple Cereal

Makes 6 servings

This cereal is crunchy and satisfying. It makes a great meal any time of day.

2 cups almond pulp (from Almond Milk, page 31)

2 apples, chopped

1/4 cup raisins

1 tablespoon ground cinnamon

2 teaspoons raw agave nectar

1 teaspoon unsweetened shredded dried coconut

1/8 teaspoon ground nutmeg

1/8 teaspoon Himalayan salt

Velvety Dessert Milk (page 28), as needed

Combine the almond pulp, apples, raisins, cinnamon, agave nectar, dried coconut, nutmeg, and salt in a large bowl. Mix with your hands until evenly combined. Serve with Velvety Dessert Milk.

Nut Yogurt with Fresh Berries

See photo facing page 32.

Makes 4 servings

This nut-based yogurt is so creamy it will help you overcome any dairy cravings.

2 cups filtered water

1 cup almond pulp (from Velvety Dessert Milk, page 28)

1 cup soaked raw cashews

2 teaspoons probiotic powder

$\frac{1}{2}$ vanilla bean

1 pint (2 to 3 cups) blueberries

1 pint (about $2\frac{1}{2}$ cups) strawberries, stems removed

Combine the water, almond pulp, cashews, probiotic powder, and vanilla bean in a blender, and process until smooth. Pour into a glass container, and refrigerate for at least 2 hours before serving. Stored in a glass container in the refrigerator, Nut Yogurt will keep for about 4 days. Serve with the fresh berries.

Scrambled "Eggs"

Makes 2 servings

If you are craving eggs, this really hits the spot. It's always a favorite dish at parties.

3 ripe Hass or Reed avocados
Himalayan salt
Freshly ground black pepper

*P*lace the avocado flesh in a bowl. Lightly mash it with a fork, but maintain some of the texture. Season with salt and pepper to taste.

Happy Porridge

Makes 2 servings

This raw porridge makes an excellent alternative to cooked oatmeal.

1 cup pecan pulp (from Pecan Milk, page 34)
½ cup raisins
½ cup unsweetened shredded dried coconut
1 teaspoon raw agave nectar
½ teaspoon ground cinnamon
⅛ teaspoon Himalayan salt
½ cup Pecan Milk (page 34)

Combine the pecan pulp, raisins, coconut, agave nectar, cinnamon, and salt in a large bowl. Mix with your hands until evenly combined. Pour the Pecan Milk over each serving.

Appetizers

Cucumber Pizzas

Makes 4 servings

See photo facing page 33.

One day I was in a hurry to prepare something tasty before one of my friends came over for tea, but all I had in the house were olives and cucumbers. Hence this recipe was born. My friend loved it and requests it every time she comes to visit.

4 cucumbers, sliced into rounds
2 cups chopped raw olives

*A*rrange the cucumber slices on an attractive serving platter. Top with the chopped olives and serve.

Going Nuts Pâté Rolls

Makes 3 servings

See photo facing page 33.

This pâté is savory and satisfying.

2 cups almond pulp (from Almond Milk, page 31)

1/4 cup chopped fresh parsley

1/4 cup chopped fresh cilantro

1/4 cup minced sweet onions

3 tablespoons nutritional yeast powder

1 tablespoon raw hempseed oil

1 teaspoon Himalayan salt

3 small romaine leaves

3 pitted Italian olives

Combine the almond pulp, parsley, cilantro, onions, nutritional yeast powder, hempseed oil, and salt in a food processor, and pulse until the ingredients are well chopped. Divide equally among the romaine leaves, and roll up the leaves burrito-style. Use a toothpick to hold each roll together, and place an olive on the end of each toothpick.

Stuffed Avocados

Makes 3 servings

My husband came up with this dish when he was craving Mexican food. Everyone went wild over it!

3 ripe avocados
2 ripe tomatoes, diced
1 bell pepper, diced
½ red onion, finely chopped
Cayenne
Chili powder
Himalayan salt
Freshly ground black pepper
Lettuce
3 sprigs fresh cilantro

Slice the avocados in half lengthwise, twist to separate the halves, and remove the pits. Carefully scoop out the flesh with a spoon, and place it in a bowl. Set the avocado shells aside.

Mash the avocado flesh. Add the tomatoes, bell pepper, and onion. Season with cayenne, chili powder, salt, and pepper to taste, and mix well. Spoon into the reserved avocado shells. Arrange a bed of lettuce on an attractive serving platter. Place the stuffed shells on the lettuce, and garnish with the cilantro sprigs.

Avocado Boats

Makes 3 servings

Your guests will be delighted when you serve this imaginative dish.

6 ripe avocados
4 ripe mangoes
2 ripe tomatoes, sliced in half
1/2 sweet onion
1/2 cup chopped fresh cilantro
1 teaspoon Himalayan salt
1/2 jalapeño chile
1/2 teaspoon Mexican seasoning

Slice the avocados in half lengthwise, twist to separate the halves, and remove the pits. Carefully scoop out the flesh with a spoon, and place it in a food processor. Set the avocado shells aside.

Peel the mango and slice the flesh from the seed. Place the mango flesh in the food processor with the avocado and add the tomatoes, onion, cilantro, salt, chile, and Mexican seasoning, and pulse to chop. Divide the mixture equally among the avocado shells and serve.

Stuffed Mushrooms

Makes 3 servings

See photo facing page 33.

These mushrooms make an elegant appetizer and will spice up any party.

1 pound (16 ounces) fresh mushrooms

1 bell pepper, diced

1 cup pitted raw olives

1 tablespoon extra-virgin olive oil

2 tablespoons minced fresh basil

1½ tablespoons freshly squeezed lemon juice

⅛ teaspoon freshly ground black pepper

Clean the mushrooms. Carefully remove the stems and set the caps aside. Place the stems in a food processor along with the bell pepper, olives, olive oil, basil, lemon juice, and black pepper, and pulse to chop. Divide the mixture equally among the mushroom caps and serve.

Heavenly Salads

Junk Food Salad

Makes 3 servings

This salad tastes surprisingly like barbecue-flavored potato chips.

1 pound (16 ounces) organic salad mix
2 tablespoons freshly squeezed lemon juice
2 tablespoons raw hempseed oil
1 tablespoon onion powder
1 teaspoon Himalayan salt
1/4 teaspoon dried tarragon
Pinch of cayenne

Place the salad mix in a large bowl and add the remaining ingredients. Toss gently until the seasonings are evenly distributed. Serve immediately.

On the Orient

See photo facing page 65.

Makes 3 servings

Are you in the mood for Chinese food?

SALAD MIX

1 cup shredded Chinese cabbage

1 cup shredded romaine lettuce

1 cup mung bean sprouts

$\frac{1}{2}$ cup trimmed snow peas

$\frac{1}{4}$ cup chopped broccoli

$\frac{1}{4}$ cup thinly sliced carrots

$\frac{1}{4}$ cup sliced celery

DRESSING

3 tablespoons freshly squeezed lemon juice

1 tablespoon Nama Shoyu

2 tablespoons filtered water

$\frac{1}{4}$ teaspoon minced fresh garlic

$\frac{1}{4}$ teaspoon minced fresh ginger

Combine all of the salad ingredients in a large bowl, and toss gently. Place the dressing ingredients in a blender, and process until well combined. Pour the dressing over the salad ingredients, and toss until evenly distributed.

Divine Fruit Salad

Makes 3 servings

This is my favorite fruit salad, hands down! The combination of fruits used in this marvelous dish creates a lovely marriage of flavors.

1½ cups (about 8 ounces) fresh strawberries, stems removed
2 tangerines or Mandarin oranges
2 kiwis
1½ cups (about 8 ounces) fresh blueberries
¼ cup freshly squeezed orange juice
1 tablespoon raw agave nectar

Wash all the fruit and pat it dry. Chop the strawberries, tangerines, and kiwis into bite-size pieces. Place in a large bowl and add the blueberries. Toss gently. Add the orange juice and agave nectar, and toss gently until evenly combined.

Greek Salad

Makes 3 servings

This hearty salad is divine.

4 ripe tomatoes, chopped
2 cucumbers, sliced or chopped
1 bell pepper, chopped
1/2 red onion, chopped
2 tablespoons extra-virgin olive oil
2 tablespoons freshly squeezed lemon juice
8 raw olives
1 garlic clove, minced

Combine the tomatoes, cucumbers, bell pepper, and onion in a large bowl. Add the olive oil, lemon juice, olives, and garlic, and toss well.

Hey, It's Raita!

Makes 3 servings

This tasty combination makes a light and refreshing salad.

5 ripe tomatoes, chopped

4 cucumbers, chopped

1 red onion, chopped

2 tablespoons freshly squeezed lemon juice

1 tablespoon raw tahini

Himalayan salt

Freshly ground black pepper

Ground cumin

Combine the tomatoes, cucumbers, and red onion in a large bowl. Add the lemon juice and tahini and mix well. Season with salt, pepper, and cumin to taste.

Fashionable Carrot and Raisin Salad

Makes 3 servings

This salad is a favorite with children of all ages.

SALAD MIX
3 cups grated carrots
1/2 cup raisins
1 apple, finely chopped
2 celery stalks, finely chopped
1/4 cup raw walnuts, finely chopped

DRESSING
1 cup Dreamy Sour Cream (page 70)
1/4 cup freshly squeezed orange juice
1/8 teaspoon Himalayan salt

Combine the salad ingredients in a large bowl, and toss until evenly distributed. Place the dressing ingredients in a small bowl, and stir until smooth and well combined. Pour the dressing over the carrot salad and mix well.

Wild Greens with Ginger Dressing

Makes 3 servings

Wild greens doused with a ginger-infused dressing are rich in nutrients and flavor.

SALAD MIX

1/2 pound (8 ounces) spring mix

2 Roma tomatoes, diced

GINGER DRESSING

1/2 cup raw hempseed oil

5 tablespoons raw agave nectar

1 tablespoon Nama Shoyu

4 tablespoons freshly squeezed lemon juice

1 teaspoon onion powder

1/4-inch slice fresh ginger

1/8 teaspoon cayenne

Combine the spring mix and tomatoes in a large bowl. Place the hempseed oil, agave nectar, Nama Shoyu, lemon juice, onion powder, ginger, and cayenne in a blender, and process until well combined. Pour over the salad mix and toss gently.

Wild Greens and Raspberries

Makes 3 servings

See photo between pages 96-97.

This is a very elegant and delicious dish.

2³⁄4 cups (about 12 ounces) fresh raspberries
1⁄3 cup extra-virgin olive oil
4 tablespoons freshly squeezed lemon juice
1 garlic clove
1⁄2 teaspoon raw agave nectar
1⁄4 teaspoon whole mustard seeds
Himalayan salt
Freshly ground black pepper
1⁄2 pound (8 ounces) spring mix

Combine the raspberries, olive oil, lemon juice, garlic clove, agave nectar, mustard seeds, and salt and pepper to taste in a blender, and process until smooth. Place the spring mix in a salad bowl. Pour the raspberry dressing over the spring mix, and toss gently.

Caesar's Delight

Makes 3 servings

I devised this dish to impress all the Caesar salad lovers in my family.

1/2 cup extra-virgin olive oil
1/2 cup freshly squeezed lemon juice
15 pitted raw olives
1/3 cup chopped sweet onions
1 tablespoon unpasteurized miso
1 tablespoon raw tahini
1 garlic clove
1/2 teaspoon Himalayan salt
1/2 teaspoon freshly ground black pepper
1/4 teaspoon fresh oregano
10 to 12 cups sliced romaine lettuce

Combine the olive oil, lemon juice, olives, onions, miso, tahini, garlic, salt, pepper, and oregano in a blender, and process until smooth. Pour over the romaine lettuce, and toss gently until evenly distributed.

Sprouts 'n' Greens Salad

Makes 2 servings

Sprouts are the elixir of life. Not only is this salad good for you, it's delicious.

1 cup spring mix
1 cup sunflower sprouts
1 cup clover sprouts
1/2 cup broccoli sprouts
3 tablespoons raw hempseed oil
2 tablespoons freshly squeezed lemon juice
1/2 teaspoon Himalayan salt
1/4 teaspoon freshly ground black pepper
1/4 teaspoon cayenne
1/4 teaspoon chopped jalapeño chile

Combine all the ingredients in a large bowl, and toss gently until well combined.

Corn and Cherry Tomato Salad

Makes 3 servings

This salad is so much fun to eat. It really excites the palate.

1 package (10 ounces) frozen organic corn

1/2 pound (8 ounces) cherry tomatoes (25 to 35 tomatoes)

1/2 cup chopped fresh cilantro

1 tablespoon extra-virgin olive oil

1 teaspoon Himalayan salt

1/2 teaspoon freshly ground black pepper

1/4 teaspoon cayenne

*P*lace the corn in a strainer and run hot water over it until thawed. Drain and transfer to a large bowl. Add the remaining ingredients to the bowl and mix well.

The Garden Salad

Makes 1 serving

With this Greek salad, simplicity meets tasty.

¼ head red leaf lettuce, torn
¼ head romaine lettuce, torn
½ Roma tomato, in wedges
⅛ cucumber, thinly sliced
¼ ripe avocado, thinly sliced
¼ carrot, thinly sliced
2 tablespoons extra-virgin olive oil
2 teaspoons freshly squeezed lemon juice

Combine all the ingredients in a bowl, and toss gently. Serve the salad immediately.

Soups

Cream of Zucchini Soup

Makes 1 serving

This creamy, rich soup is delicious and elegant.

1 cup chopped zucchinis

1 ripe avocado

1/2 cup chopped celery

1/2 cup filtered water

1 tablespoon extra-virgin olive oil

1 tablespoon freshly squeezed lemon juice

1 teaspoon dried dill weed

1 garlic clove

1/4 teaspoon Himalayan salt

Combine all the ingredients in a blender, and process until smooth. Serve immediately.

Note: This recipe can be doubled and served as an impressive appetizer for a party.

Hot! Hot! Hot!
Aguacate Soup

Makes 3 servings *See photo facing page 64.*

*Aguacate means "avocado" in Spanish. This unusual
Mexican soup gets its heat from fresh ginger, onion,
and cayenne.*

5 ripe avocados

2 ripe tomatoes

4 celery stalks, coarsely chopped

$1/2$ sweet onion

$1/2$ cup chopped fresh cilantro

3 to 4 tablespoons freshly squeezed lemon juice

$1/4$-inch slice fresh ginger

Himalayan salt

Cayenne

*P*lace the avocados, tomatoes, celery, onion, cilantro, lemon juice,
and ginger in a blender, and process until smooth. Season with salt
and cayenne to taste, and blend again briefly. Serve immediately.

*H*erb-Infused Soup

Makes 3 servings

Here's a fun way to use up herbs that are left over from other recipes. It is amazingly satisfying.

1 cup filtered water

1/2 cup young coconut water

1/2 cup chopped fresh cilantro

1/4 cup Nama Shoyu

1/4 cup fresh basil

1/4 cup fresh tarragon

1/4 cup fresh oregano

2 tablespoons extra-virgin olive oil

2 tablespoons freshly squeezed lemon juice

1 1/2 tablespoons raw agave nectar

2 garlic cloves

1 teaspoon fresh thyme

1 teaspoon fresh rosemary

1/2 teaspoon Himalayan salt

*C*ombine all the ingredients in a blender, and process until smooth.

Hot! Hot! Hot! Aguacate Soup, page 63
Crème Tomat, page 67
Zippy "Tuna" Rolls, page 84

Corn Symphony

Makes 2 servings

This deeply satisfying soup is chock-full of Mexican flavor.

2 packages (10 ounces each) frozen organic corn

2 cups Almond Milk (page 31)

1/2 cup chopped fresh cilantro

1/2 red bell pepper

1/2 jalapeño chile

1 teaspoon Himalayan salt

1/8 teaspoon freshly ground black pepper

*P*lace the corn in a strainer and run hot water over it until thawed. Drain and transfer to a blender. Add the remaining ingredients to the blender, and process until smooth.

Note: You can adjust the heat by adding more or less jalapeño chile. If you are sensitive to spicy food, omit the jalapeño chile.

On the Orient, page 49

Crème a la Mushroom

Makes 3 servings

This soup is delightful, flavorful, and easy to make.

1 cup whole cremini mushrooms

2 cups Almond Milk (page 31)

1/2 cup finely chopped celery

1/4 cup chopped fresh parsley

1 tablespoon raw almond butter

1 teaspoon Himalayan salt

1 teaspoon extra-virgin olive oil

1/8 teaspoon freshly ground black pepper

Clean the mushrooms, and place them into a blender whole. Add the remaining ingredients, and process until smooth.

Crème Tomat

Makes 3 servings

See photo facing page 64.

What a blessing this soup is. I practically lived on tomato soup when I was a kid, and this soup always satisfies that craving.

3 large ripe tomatoes

1 cup Almond Milk (page 31)

1 ripe avocado

$1/2$ cup fresh basil

$1/4$ cup fresh oregano

1 teaspoon Himalayan salt

1 teaspoon curry powder

1 teaspoon freshly squeezed lemon juice

$1/4$ teaspoon ground cumin

$1/8$ teaspoon freshly ground black pepper

Combine all the ingredients in a blender, and process until smooth.

Sauces

Dreamy Sour Cream

Makes 3 servings

You will be amazed by this sour cream. I used to cater large parties, and this was my most requested topping.

1 cup soaked raw sunflower seeds
3/4 cup plus 1 tablespoon filtered water
1 teaspoon probiotic powder
1/2 cup peeled and chopped cucumbers
1/4 sweet onion
1/4 cup chopped celery
1/2 lemon, peeled, seeded, and coarsely chopped
2 small garlic cloves (do not peel)
1/4 teaspoon Himalayan salt

*P*lace the sunflower seeds in a blender. Add 3/4 cup of the water, and process until creamy. Add the probiotic powder and blend again. Add the remaining 1 tablespoon water, cucumber, onion, celery, lemon, garlic cloves, and salt. Process until completely smooth.

Note: Add more or less water to achieve the desired consistency.

Sexy Salsa

Makes 3 servings

This salsa is bursting with flavor and healthful antioxidants.

1 cup finely chopped tomatoes
1/2 cup chopped fresh cilantro
1/4 cup chopped sweet onions
1/4 cup chopped jalapeño chiles
2 teaspoons chopped fresh basil
1/2-inch slice fresh ginger
1 garlic clove
Himalayan salt

Combine the tomatoes, cilantro, onions, chiles, basil, ginger, and garlic in a food processor, and pulse to chop. Season with salt to taste.

Cultured Ranch Dressing

Makes 4 servings

I created this dressing for my husband, a ranch dressing fanatic.

2 1/2 cups Nut Yogurt (page 37), vanilla bean omitted

1 1/2 cups young coconut water

3 to 4 tablespoons freshly squeezed lemon juice

3 garlic cloves

2 teaspoons Himalayan salt

1/8 teaspoon freshly ground black pepper

Combine all the ingredients in a blender, and process until smooth.

Mind-Blowing Dressing

Makes 3 servings

This recipe was developed by my mom. It will blow your mind!

4 tablespoons freshly squeezed lemon juice

2 tablespoons extra-virgin olive oil

2 garlic cloves, pressed

$\frac{1}{2}$ teaspoon dried tarragon

$\frac{1}{2}$ teaspoon Italian seasoning

$\frac{1}{2}$ teaspoon Himalayan salt

$\frac{1}{2}$ teaspoon freshly ground black pepper

Combine all the ingredients in a jar. Seal tightly, and shake until well blended.

Note: This dressing is fabulous on almost every type of salad imaginable. If you put it in the freezer for a while, it will become very firm and will make a delectable buttery spread. The dressing may also be used to marinate sun-dried tomatoes and mushrooms.

_H_appy Dressing

Makes 3 servings

I developed this recipe when I had just a few ingredients in the house. I was so impressed I decided to name it Happy Dressing. Pour it over salad greens, or serve it as a dip with carrots.

2/3 cup filtered water

4 tablespoons freshly squeezed lemon juice

3 tablespoons raw tahini

2 tablespoons nutritional yeast powder

1 teaspoon Himalayan salt

1/2 teaspoon raw agave nectar

1/4 teaspoon freshly ground black pepper

1/8 teaspoon cayenne

Combine all the ingredients in a bowl, and stir until well blended.

Satay Sauce

Makes 3 servings

*When I was growing up, I was addicted to satay sauce.
I wanted it with every meal. I developed this recipe to satisfy
that craving. Where are the peanuts? I thought it would be
fun to create a satay sauce without peanuts so everyone
could enjoy it. Pour it over salad greens, or use it as a dip
for raw vegetables.*

3 to 4 tablespoons freshly squeezed orange juice

2 tablespoons raw tahini

2 tablespoons unpasteurized miso

1 teaspoon nutritional yeast powder

1 teaspoon Nama Shoyu

1 teaspoon raw agave nectar

$\frac{1}{2}$ teaspoon cayenne

Combine all the ingredients in a bowl, and stir until well blended.

Presto Pesto!

Makes 3 servings

If you have soaked sunflower seeds on hand, you can prepare this exquisite pesto in under five minutes. It makes a delicious quick dipping sauce for vegetables, or use it in Angelina's Easy Lasagne (page 94) or Presto Pesto Linguine (page 101).

1 cup fresh basil

$1/3$ cup extra-virgin olive oil

3 to 4 tablespoons freshly squeezed lemon juice

1 teaspoon Himalayan salt

$3^1/2$ cups soaked raw sunflower seeds

$1/8$ teaspoon freshly ground black pepper

$1/8$ teaspoon cayenne

$\mathcal{P}$lace the basil, olive oil, lemon juice, and salt in a food processor, and pulse to chop. Add the sunflower seeds, black pepper, and cayenne, and pulse again until evenly combined. Transfer to an attractive bowl and serve.

Note: Be sure to soak the sunflower seeds for 3 hours before making the pesto.

Olive Medley

Makes 3 servings

*This sensational olive pâté is marvelously robust! Use it
as a topping for Angelina's Easy Lasagne (page 94)
or as a tapenade with raw crackers.*

1½ cups pitted raw olives
1 red bell pepper, diced

Place the olives and red bell pepper in a food processor, and pulse
until evenly chopped.

Delightful Entrées

*C*elestial Fettuccine Alfredo

Makes 3 servings

This dish was created by accident, but it has proven to be one of my most successful recipes. It is awesome!

ZUCCHINI FETTUCCINE
8 young zucchinis

ALFREDO SAUCE
2$\frac{1}{2}$ cups walnut pulp (from Luscious Walnut Milk, page 111)
2 teaspoons Himalayan salt
1 garlic clove (do not peel)
$\frac{1}{2}$ teaspoon ground nutmeg
$\frac{1}{4}$ teaspoon dried oregano
Freshly ground black pepper
Parsley, for garnish

ITALIAN BRUSCHETTA SAUCE
5 Roma tomatoes, diced
1 cup finely chopped fresh basil
$\frac{1}{2}$ cup finely chopped fresh tarragon
2 tablespoons freshly squeezed lemon juice
1 teaspoon Himalayan salt
Extra-virgin olive oil

PARMESAN CHEESE
1 cup raw pine nuts
1/4 cup nutritional yeast powder
1/2 teaspoon Himalayan salt
1/2 teaspoon dried oregano

For the fettuccine: Using a vegetable peeler or spiral slicer, cut the zucchinis into long, thin strips to create vegetable "noodles." Set aside.

For the alfredo sauce: Combine the walnut pulp, salt, garlic, nutmeg, oregano, and pepper to taste in a blender, and process until smooth. Set aside.

For the bruschetta sauce: Combine the tomatoes, basil, tarragon, lemon juice, and salt in a bowl. Drizzle with enough olive oil to evenly coat the top.

For the Parmesan cheese: Combine the pine nuts, nutritional yeast powder, salt, and oregano in a food processor, and pulse until finely ground.

To assemble: Pour the alfredo sauce over the zucchini strips, and toss until evenly distributed. Top with the bruschetta sauce and Parmesan cheese, and garnish with parsley.

Fiesta Tacos

Makes 3 servings

I love Mexican food, and so I created this enticing recipe.

TACO SHELLS

2 romaine hearts, leaves separated

MEXICAN PÂTÉ

2 cups soaked raw sunflower seeds

1 cup sun-dried tomatoes, soaked for 15 minutes

2 tablespoons Mexican seasoning

1 tablespoon unpasteurized miso

1 teaspoon Himalayan salt

1 teaspoon cayenne

AVOCADO, JICAMA, AND CORN MEDLEY

2 packages (10 ounces each) frozen organic corn

1 ripe avocado, chopped

1 jicama, peeled and chopped

3 to 4 tablespoons freshly squeezed lemon juice

1/2 teaspoon Himalayan salt

1/4 teaspoon cayenne

TOPPINGS

1 recipe Dreamy Sour Cream (page 70)

1 recipe Sexy Salsa (page 71)

For the taco shells: Wash and dry the romaine leaves, and set aside.

For the pâté: Place the sunflower seeds, sun-dried tomatoes, Mexican seasoning, miso, salt, and cayenne in a food processor, and process until well combined.

For the medley: Place the corn in a strainer and run hot water over it until thawed. Drain and transfer to a bowl. Add the avocado, jicama, lemon juice, salt, and cayenne, and mix well.

To assemble: Spoon the pâté equally on each of the romaine leaves. Spoon the medley over the pâté. Top with Dreamy Sour Cream and Sexy Salsa, and serve.

Zippy "Tuna" Rolls

Makes 3 servings

See photo facing page 64.

If you like sushi, you are going to love these!

1$\frac{1}{2}$ cups soaked raw sunflower seeds

$\frac{1}{2}$ cup chopped fresh dill weed

$\frac{1}{2}$ sweet onion

2 celery stalks, chopped

1 heirloom tomato, coarsely chopped

3 to 4 tablespoons freshly squeezed lemon juice

$\frac{1}{2}$ jalapeño chile

1 teaspoon Himalayan salt

1 teaspoon extra-virgin olive oil

Freshly ground black pepper

$\frac{1}{2}$ cup bell peppers, chopped into matchsticks (optional)

$\frac{1}{2}$ cup peeled cucumber, chopped into matchsticks (optional)

6 sheets raw nori

Lettuce

Combine the sunflower seeds, dill weed, onion, celery, tomato, lemon juice, chile, salt, olive oil, and pepper to taste in a food processor, and pulse until evenly chopped but still slightly chunky. Carefully spread the mixture evenly over each nori sheet, roll them up, and slice into 1½-inch pieces. Arrange the pieces on a bed of lettuce and serve.

Note: To make these rolls more like traditional sushi rolls, place one or two bell pepper and cucumber matchsticks on the mixture before rolling up the nori sheet.

Rawsome Italiano

See photo facing page 96.

I highly recommend serving this dish to impress a loved one.

MARINARA SAUCE

6 Roma tomatoes

1/2 cup sun-dried tomatoes, soaked for 15 minutes

1/2 cup chopped fresh basil

1 green onion, chopped

2 tablespoons extra-virgin olive oil

1 teaspoon Nama Shoyu

1 garlic clove

1/2 teaspoon raw agave nectar

Himalayan salt

Freshly ground black pepper

Dried oregano

ZUCCHINI SPAGHETTI WITH VEGETABLES

1 zucchini
1/4 red bell pepper, chopped
1/5 sweet onion, chopped
8 pitted raw olives, sliced
Himalayan salt
Freshly ground black pepper
1/2 teaspoon chopped fresh parsley, for garnish

For the sauce: Slice the Roma tomatoes in half, and place them in a blender. Add the sun-dried tomatoes, basil, green onion, olive oil, Nama Shoyu, garlic, agave nectar, and salt, pepper, and oregano to taste. Process until smooth.

For the spaghetti: Using a vegetable peeler or spiral slicer, cut the zucchini into long, thin strips to create vegetable "spaghetti." Add the red bell pepper, onion, olives, and salt and pepper to taste, and toss gently. Pour the sauce on top, and garnish with the parsley.

Pasta Marinara

Makes 2 servings

This marinara sauce is rich in flavor and deeply satisfying. It's the perfect topping for vegetable "noodles."

2 large zucchinis
1 red bell pepper, chopped
$\frac{1}{2}$ cup sun-dried tomatoes, soaked for 15 minutes
1 tablespoon Italian seasoning
1 garlic clove
$\frac{1}{2}$ teaspoon raw agave nectar
$\frac{1}{8}$ teaspoon freshly ground black pepper
$\frac{1}{8}$ teaspoon cayenne
Himalayan salt

Using a vegetable peeler or spiral slicer, cut the zucchinis into long, thin strips to create vegetable "noodles." Set aside.

Combine the red bell pepper, sun-dried tomatoes, Italian seasoning, garlic, agave nectar, black pepper, cayenne, and salt to taste in a blender, and process until smooth. Pour over the zucchini strips and serve.

Stuffed Peppers

Makes 3 servings

This raw version of stuffed peppers is outstanding.

2 cups soaked raw sunflower seeds

1 cup sun-dried tomatoes, soaked

1/4 cup chopped fresh cilantro

2 tablespoons Mexican seasoning

1 tablespoon unpasteurized miso

1 teaspoon cayenne

1 teaspoon Himalayan salt

1 garlic clove, minced

3 red bell peppers

Romaine lettuce leaves

Combine the sunflower seeds, sun-dried tomatoes, cilantro, Mexican seasoning, miso, cayenne, salt, and garlic in a food processor, and process until smooth. Slice off the tops of the red bell peppers, and remove the seeds. Stuff the peppers with the pâté, and serve on a bed of romaine lettuce.

Broccoli in Cheese Sauce

Makes 2 servings

This is profoundly creamy and cheesy-tasting.

---

1 bunch broccoli

6 tablespoons raw tahini

1 tablespoon nutritional yeast powder

$1/2$ teaspoon Himalayan salt

$1/4$ teaspoon cayenne

Clean the broccoli, trim the stems, and slice it into bite-size pieces. Combine the tahini, nutritional yeast powder, salt, and cayenne in a large bowl. Add the broccoli and mix well.

Starry Cucumbers and Avocado Extraordinaire

Makes 3 servings

This recipe was created in honor of the summer solstice. It's wonderful!

5 ripe avocados, cubed

4 cucumbers, chopped

3 Roma tomatoes, chopped

1/2 sweet onion, chopped

1/4 cup chopped fresh chives

2 fresh parsley sprigs, chopped

2 tablespoons raw tahini

2 tablespoons freshly squeezed lemon juice

1 teaspoon extra-virgin olive oil

1/4 jalapeño chile, chopped

Himalayan salt

Freshly ground black pepper

Combine the avocados, cucumbers, tomatoes, onion, chives, parsley, tahini, lemon juice, olive oil, and chile in a large bowl. Mix well. Season with salt and pepper to taste, and mix again.

Spinach and Walnut Pie in a Flash

Makes 6 pieces

If you like potpies and quiche, this dish is bound to become a favorite.

2 cups fresh spinach, chopped

$\frac{1}{2}$ cup raw cashews

$\frac{1}{4}$ cup filtered water

2 tablespoons ground flaxseeds

2 cups raw walnuts

Combine the spinach, cashews, water, and flaxseeds in a blender, and process until smooth. Set aside.

Grind the walnuts in a food processor. Press the ground walnuts into a glass pie pan to form a crust. Pour the blended ingredients into the pie crust. Let rest for 25–30 minutes before serving.

Noodle Supreme

Makes 3 servings

You won't believe how delicious this is!

3 young coconuts
1 cup freshly squeezed orange juice
1 cup raw tahini
1 tablespoon Nama Shoyu
6 pitted dates, soaked for 10–15 minutes
1 teaspoon raw agave nectar
1/4-inch slice fresh ginger
1 cup snow peas
1/2 cup chopped bok choy
1/2 cup chopped Chinese cabbage
1/3 cup raw sesame seeds

Cut open the coconuts, pour out the coconut water (save it for another recipe), and scrape out the coconut meat. Slice the coconut meat into noodle strips and set aside.

Place the orange juice, tahini, Nama Shoyu, dates, agave nectar, and ginger in a blender, and process until smooth.

Combine the coconut noodles, snow peas, bok choy, and Chinese cabbage in a serving bowl. Add the blended ingredients and mix well. Top with the sesame seeds.

A ngelina's Easy Lasagne

Makes 8 servings

See photo between pages 96-97.

Serve this at a party and you will wow everyone. This recipe takes longer than five minutes and requires some advance preparation, but it's well worth a little extra time.

$1/2$ cup extra-virgin olive oil

3 to 4 tablespoons freshly squeezed lemon juice

1 teaspoon Himalayan salt

$1/2$ teaspoon Italian seasoning

$1/2$ teaspoon freshly ground black pepper

$1/8$ teaspoon cayenne

2 packages (12 ounces each) frozen artichoke hearts, thawed

1 recipe Presto Pesto (page 76)

4 large ripe tomatoes, sliced

$1/4$ cup minced fresh basil

1 recipe Olive Medley (page 78)

2 tablespoons nutritional yeast powder

Combine the olive oil, lemon juice, salt, Italian seasoning, black pepper, and cayenne in a bowl. Add the artichoke hearts, stir gently, and set aside to marinate for 1 hour.

Line the bottom of a 13 x 9 x 2-inch casserole dish with the Presto Pesto. Tear apart each marinated artichoke heart to make "noodles," and place over the pesto. Layer the tomatoes over the artichokes, completely covering them. Scatter the basil over the tomatoes. Distribute the Olive Medley evenly over the basil. Sprinkle with the nutritional yeast powder and additional salt and pepper to taste. Serve immediately.

Note: This lasagne goes beautifully with Greek Salad (page 51).

Corn Medley

Makes 3 servings

Corn aficionados will fall in love with this recipe.

2 packages (12 ounces each) frozen organic corn
3 ripe tomatoes, diced
2 ripe avocados, diced
2 bell peppers, diced
$1/2$ cup finely chopped fresh cilantro
$1/4$ cup extra-virgin olive oil
3 to 4 tablespoons freshly squeezed lemon juice
1 teaspoon Himalayan salt
$1/8$ teaspoon cayenne
$1/8$ teaspoon chili powder
$1/8$ teaspoon garlic powder

*P*lace the corn in a strainer and run hot water over it until thawed. Drain and transfer to a large bowl. Add the remaining ingredients, and toss gently.

facing this page: *Rawsome Italiano, page 86*

following page: *Lemon Pudding, page 113*
Chocolate Pudding, page 119

A sian Cabbage

Makes 3 servings

This dish is not only delicious, it is quick to prepare.

1 medium head napa cabbage, thinly sliced
4 ripe tomatoes, sliced
$^1/_2$ cup raw cashews, chopped
1 carrot, thinly sliced
$^1/_4$ cup mung bean sprouts
$^1/_4$ cup cold-pressed sesame oil
$^1/_4$ cup raw tahini
1 tablespoon Nama Shoyu
$^1/_2$-inch slice fresh ginger
$^1/_2$ teaspoon raw agave nectar

Combine the cabbage, tomatoes, cashews, carrot, and sprouts in a large bowl. Place the sesame oil, tahini, Nama Shoyu, ginger, and agave nectar in a blender, and process until smooth. Pour over the cabbage mixture, and toss until evenly distributed.

facing this page: *Tostada Fun, page 98*

previous page: *Wild Greens and Raspberries, page 56*
Angelina's Easy Lasagne, page 94

Tostada Fun

Makes 3 servings

See photo facing page 97.

*Friends and family will enjoy eating this tasty and fun
Mexican dish.*

½ head cabbage
3 ripe avocados, cubed
3 ripe tomatoes, chopped
1 red bell pepper, chopped
¼ onion, chopped
½ jalapeño chile, chopped
1 teaspoon nutritional yeast powder
1 teaspoon Himalayan salt
½ teaspoon Mexican seasoning
⅛ teaspoon freshly ground black pepper
1 recipe Sexy Salsa (page 71)
½ cup clover sprouts

Carefully separate the cabbage leaves to make individual bowls.
Place the avocados, tomatoes, bell pepper, onion, and chile in a bowl.
Add the nutritional yeast powder, salt, Mexican seasoning, and black
pepper, and mix thoroughly. Spoon the avocado mixture into the cabbage bowls, and top with the Sexy Salsa and sprouts.

Happy Thai

Makes 3 servings

This is a fun Thai recipe that is sure to please everyone.

1½ cups chopped broccoli

1 red bell pepper, diced

1 green bell pepper, diced

1 yellow bell pepper, diced

1 cup frozen green peas, thawed

1 cup young coconut water

1 cup young coconut meat

1 tablespoon Nama Shoyu

2 tablespoons raw tahini

2 tablespoons freshly squeezed lemon juice

½-inch slice fresh ginger

½ teaspoon chili powder

½ teaspoon ground turmeric

½ teaspoon raw agave nectar

Combine the broccoli, bell peppers, and peas in a bowl. Combine the coconut water, coconut meat, Nama Shoyu, tahini, lemon juice, ginger, chili powder, turmeric, and agave nectar in a blender, and process until smooth. Pour the blended mixture over the vegetables, and toss until well combined.

Unbelievable Chili

Makes 4 servings

Even the most discerning chili lover is sure to like this recipe.

1½ cups sun-dried tomatoes

3 cups chopped avocados

1½ cups raw almonds

2 ripe tomatoes, chopped

½ cup chopped carrots

½ cup chopped fresh cilantro

½ cup freshly squeezed lemon juice

1 tablespoon chili powder

½ jalapeño chile, diced

1 tablespoon ground cumin

1 teaspoon Himalayan salt

⅛ teaspoon freshly ground black pepper

Soak the sun-dried tomatoes in enough water to cover for at least 15 minutes. Do not drain. Transfer the sun-dried tomatoes and the soak water to a blender. Add the remaining ingredients, and pulse the blender briefly, just until the ingredients are chopped and mixed. The texture should be thick and chunky.

Note: For a treat, top the chili with Dreamy Sour Cream (page 70).

Ian's Avo Rockets

Makes 3 servings

My son Ian, the raw teen, created this to impress his friends.

2 ripe avocados
2 sheets raw nori
Lettuce

Slice the avocados into crescent moons, and peel off the skin. Slice the nori into ¼-inch-thick strips, and wrap them around each avocado slice. Serve on a bed of lettuce.

Presto Pesto Linguine

Makes 3 servings

This heavily requested dish tastes surprisingly authentic.

4 zucchinis
1 recipe Presto Pesto (page 76)

Using a vegetable peeler or spiral slicer, cut the zucchinis into long, thin strips to create vegetable "linguine." Top with the pesto, and toss until evenly distributed.

Spaghetti with Aïoli Sauce

Makes 3 servings

Garlic lovers will ask for this again and again.

4 zucchinis

¼ cup extra-virgin olive oil

3 to 4 tablespoons freshly squeezed lemon juice

1 teaspoon Himalayan salt

3 small garlic cloves

½ teaspoon Italian seasoning

⅛ teaspoon freshly ground black pepper

Using a vegetable peeler or spiral slicer, cut the zucchinis into long, thin strips to create vegetable "spaghetti." Combine the olive oil, lemon juice, salt, garlic, Italian seasoning, and black pepper in a blender, and process until smooth. Pour over the zucchini strips and serve.

Scrumptious Desserts

Chocolate Bliss Pudding with Coconut Cream

Makes 3 servings

This is chocolate paradise, especially when served chilled and topped with coconut cream.

COCONUT CREAM

3 young coconuts, meat only

Water from 1 young coconut

1 vanilla bean

$1/4$ teaspoon raw agave nectar

CHOCOLATE BLISS PUDDING

1 ripe avocado

10 pitted dates, soaked

$1/3$ cup filtered water

2 tablespoons raw carob powder

1 tablespoon raw cacao nibs

1 vanilla bean

$1/8$ teaspoon Himalayan salt

For the coconut cream: Combine the coconut meat, coconut water, vanilla bean, and agave nectar in a blender, and process until smooth and creamy. Chill thoroughly (for the best flavor).

For the pudding: Combine the avocado, dates, water, carob powder, cacao nibs, vanilla bean, and salt in a blender, and process until smooth. Chill thoroughly (for the best flavor). Serve topped with the chilled coconut cream.

Note: Depending on how sweet you want the pudding, you may need to add a little raw agave nectar or a few additional dates.

Tangerine Dream

Makes 3 servings

This ice cream is a wonderful treat for the child within.

---

2 cups Almond Milk (page 31), Luscious Walnut Milk (page 111),
    Pecan Milk (page 34), or Hempseed Milk (page 32)

2 young coconuts, meat only

$\frac{1}{2}$ cup young coconut water

2 tangerines or Mandarin oranges, peeled and seeded

$\frac{1}{2}$ cup raw agave nectar

1 tablespoon vanilla flavor

$\frac{1}{8}$ teaspoon Himalayan salt

2 tablespoons raw coconut oil

Combine the Almond Milk, coconut meat, and coconut water in a blender, and process until smooth and creamy. Let stand for 1–2 minutes. Add the oranges, agave nectar, vanilla flavor, and salt, and blend well. Add the coconut oil, and blend once more. Pour into an ice cream maker, and freeze according to the manufacturer's directions.

Cherry Walnut Ice Cream

Makes 3 servings

When cherries are blended with Walnut Milk, the result is incredible!

1 package (16 ounces) frozen organic cherries
1 cup Luscious Walnut Milk (page 111), unstrained
$\frac{1}{4}$ cup raw agave nectar
1 teaspoon vanilla flavor

Combine all the ingredients in a blender, and process until smooth. Pour into an ice cream maker, and freeze according to the manufacturer's directions.

Awesome Vanilla Ice Cream

Makes 3 servings

This was one of my first raw creations. It has turned out to be the best raw vanilla ice cream ever.

---

2 cups Almond Milk (page 31), Luscious Walnut Milk (page 111), Pecan Milk (page 34), or Hempseed Milk (page 32)

2 young coconuts, meat only

$\frac{1}{2}$ cup young coconut water

$\frac{1}{2}$ cup raw agave nectar

2 tablespoons raw coconut oil

$1\frac{1}{2}$ tablespoons vanilla flavor, or 1 vanilla bean

$\frac{1}{8}$ teaspoon Himalayan salt

Combine the Almond Milk, coconut meat, and coconut water in a blender, and process until smooth and creamy. Let stand for 1–2 minutes. Add the agave nectar, coconut oil, vanilla flavor, and salt, and process until smooth. Pour into an ice cream maker, and freeze according to the manufacturer's directions.

Screamy Chocolate Fantastic

Makes 3 servings

This is my chocolate ice cream. Everyone screams for more!

1 cup raw cacao nibs (Note: If you do not own a coffee grinder,
    replace the cacao nibs with 2$\frac{1}{2}$ tablespoons raw cacao powder.)

2 teaspoons raw carob powder

$\frac{1}{2}$ teaspoon ground cinnamon

2 cups Almond Milk (page 31), Luscious Walnut Milk (page 111),
    Pecan Milk (page 34), or Hempseed Milk (page 32)

2 young coconuts, meat only

$\frac{1}{2}$ cup young coconut water

$\frac{1}{2}$ cup raw agave nectar

1 tablespoon vanilla flavor

$\frac{1}{8}$ teaspoon Himalayan salt

2 tablespoons raw coconut oil

Grind the cacao nibs into a powder in a coffee grinder. Add the carob powder and cinnamon and grind again.

Combine the Almond Milk, coconut meat, and coconut water in a blender, and process until smooth and creamy. Let stand for 1–2 minutes. Add the powdered cacao nibs, agave nectar, vanilla flavor, and salt, and blend well. Add the coconut oil, and blend once more. Pour into an ice cream maker, and freeze according to the manufacturer's directions.

Decadent Whipped Cream and Strawberries

Makes 4 servings

I have served this many times at parties, and the whipped cream always disappears before the strawberries! The trick to getting it to taste just like dairy whipped cream is to make sure you don't oversweeten it.

3 cups walnut pulp (from Luscious Walnut Milk, page 111)
3 tablespoons raw coconut oil, warmed under hot water
    until it becomes runny
1 vanilla bean
1/3 cup raw agave nectar, as needed
Filtered water, as needed
2 cups whole strawberries

Combine the walnut pulp, coconut oil, vanilla bean, and a small amount of the agave nectar in a blender, and process until smooth and creamy. Add a small amount of water to achieve a consistency similar to whipped cream. Gradually add a little more agave nectar until you reach the desired sweetness. Chill thoroughly. Serve with the strawberries for dipping.

Luscious Walnut Milk

Makes 6 cups

This drink is fun to serve as an appetizer or as a light dessert all by itself.

5 cups filtered water
1 cup soaked raw walnuts
1$\frac{1}{2}$ tablespoons vanilla flavor
3 tablespoons raw agave nectar
$\frac{1}{8}$ teaspoon Himalayan salt

Combine the water and walnuts in a blender, and process until smooth. Strain, and set aside the pulp for another recipe. Rinse out the blender jar, and pour the milk back into it. Add the vanilla flavor, agave nectar, and salt, and process until very smooth and creamy.

Note: Save the walnut pulp to use in Celestial Fettuccine Alfredo (page 80) or Decadent Whipped Cream and Strawberries (page 110).

Tropical Pops

Makes 6 pops

These frozen fruit pops are refreshing any time of the year.
Kids love them!

2 cups freshly squeezed orange juice
1 package (8 ounces) frozen mango chunks
1 package (8 ounces) frozen pineapple chunks
2 ripe bananas

Combine all the ingredients in a blender, and process until smooth and creamy. Pour into Popsicle molds and freeze.

Lemon Pudding

Makes 3 servings

See photo between pages 9-97.

This scrumptious pudding is tart, tangy, and creamy.

1 cup soaked raw cashews

1 cup filtered water

6 tablespoons freshly squeezed lemon juice

3 tablespoons plus 1 teaspoon unsweetened shredded
    dried coconut

2 tablespoons raw agave nectar

Combine the cashews, water, lemon juice, 3 tablespoons coconut, and agave nectar in a blender, and process until smooth and creamy. Pour into individual serving dishes, and top with the remaining 1 teaspoon coconut.

$\mathcal{D}$urian

Makes 6 servings

Durian is an exotic fruit with an unusual taste. It is popular in Asia and with raw foodists. I personally love durian and could not live without it on a raw diet— or any other diet, for that matter. Yum!

1 frozen durian

$\mathcal{D}$efrost the durian. To eat the fruit, split open the shell and eat the golden pillows. Remove the seeds before eating. Durian can also be blended with young coconut water to make a pudding.

Note: When purchasing a frozen durian, look for one that is brownish-yellow. Choose one with skin that is just starting to split and is heavy for its size.

Goji Berry Pops

Makes 6 pops

Goji berries are so nutritious, it's impossible to eat too many of them.

1 cup goji berries
2 cups filtered water
1 cup freshly squeezed orange juice

*P*lace the goji berries in a bowl, and cover them with the water. Let soak in the refrigerator for 8–12 hours. Place the goji berries and their soak water in a blender. Add the orange juice, and process until smooth. Pour into Popsicle molds and freeze.

Note: The trick to making these lovely pops quickly is to always have goji berries soaking in water in your refrigerator.

Apple Pie

Makes 6 servings

This apple pie is wickedly good.

CRUST

1 cup raw walnuts

1 teaspoon vanilla flavor

½ cup pitted dates

½ teaspoon ground cinnamon

⅛ teaspoon Himalayan salt

FILLING

6 Granny Smith apples, peeled, cored, and thinly sliced

1 tablespoon freshly squeezed lemon juice

2 teaspoons ground cinnamon

1 cup pitted dates

½ cup raw agave nectar

⅛ teaspoon Himalayan salt

For the crust: Place the walnuts, vanilla flavor, dates, cinnamon, and salt in a food processor, and process until the mixture holds together and forms a dough. Press into a 9-inch glass pie pan to form a crust.

For the filling: Place the apples in a large bowl. Sprinkle with the lemon juice and 1 teaspoon of the cinnamon, and toss until evenly coated. Place the dates, agave nectar, remaining 1 teaspoon cinnamon, and salt in a blender. Add a very small amount of filtered water, just enough to facilitate blending, and process until smooth. Add to the apples, and toss until evenly distributed. Spoon into the prepared crust. To serve, cut into 6 equal wedges.

Note: For a special treat, top the pie with Awesome Vanilla Ice Cream (page 108).

Blueberry Pie

Makes 6 servings

Plump, fresh blueberries are divine. Imagine how tasty they are when made into a pie.

1 cup raw walnuts
$\frac{1}{2}$ cup pitted dates
1 teaspoon vanilla flavor
$\frac{1}{2}$ teaspoon ground cinnamon
$\frac{1}{8}$ teaspoon Himalayan salt
4 cups fresh blueberries
1 tablespoon raw agave nectar

Combine the walnuts, dates, vanilla flavor, cinnamon, and salt in a food processor, and process until the mixture holds together and forms a dough. Press into a 9-inch glass pie pan. Rinse and dry the food processor. Place the blueberries and agave nectar into the food processor, and process until puréed. Pour the purée into the prepared pie crust. Chill in the refrigerator for at least 1 hour before serving.

Chocolate Pudding

Makes 3 servings

See photo between pages 96-97.

*This luscious pudding tastes so sinfully rich that no one
will guess how healthful it is.*

$^1/_2$ cup pitted dates, soaked for 15 minutes

1 ripe avocado

2 tablespoons raw carob powder

1 tablespoon raw cacao nibs

1 tablespoon raw agave nectar

1 teaspoon vanilla flavor

$^1/_8$ teaspoon Himalayan salt

Drain the dates but reserve the soak water. Place the dates in a blender along with the remaining ingredients, adding just enough of the soak water to facilitate blending. Process until smooth. Chill the pudding in the refrigerator for 1 hour before serving.

Chocolate Shake

Makes 4 servings

Try it for yourself and taste what all the fuss is about.

1 cup raw cacao nibs (Note: If you do not own a coffee grinder,
    replace the cacao nibs with 2½ tablespoons raw cacao powder.)

2 teaspoons raw carob powder

½ teaspoon ground cinnamon

2 cups Almond Milk (page 31), Luscious Walnut Milk (page 111),
    Pecan Milk (page 34), or Hempseed Milk (page 32)

2 young coconuts, meat only

½ cup young coconut water

½ cup raw agave nectar

1 tablespoon vanilla flavor

⅛ teaspoon Himalayan salt

2 tablespoons raw coconut oil

2 cups ice cubes

Grind the cacao nibs into a powder in a coffee grinder. Add the carob powder and cinnamon and grind again.

Combine the Almond Milk, coconut meat, and coconut water in a blender, and process until smooth and creamy. Let stand for 1–2 minutes. Add the powdered cacao nibs, agave nectar, vanilla flavor, and salt, and blend well. Add the coconut oil, and blend again. Add the ice, and blend once more. Serve immediately.

Life's a Bowl of Cherries Sorbet

Makes 3 servings

This simple sorbet is enchanting.

1 package (16 ounces) frozen organic cherries
$^1/_4$ cup raw agave nectar

Combine the frozen cherries and agave nectar in a blender, and process until smooth. Pour into an ice cream maker, and freeze according to the manufacturer's directions.

Note: This sorbet will keep in the freezer for up to 3 months.

Suppliers

Frontier Natural Products
www.frontiercoop.com
PO Box 299
3021 78th Street
Norway, IA 52318
Telephone: 800-669-3275
customercare@frontiercoop.com
Spices, dried herbs, seasoning
blends, vanilla flavor.

Living Tree Community Foods
www.livingtreecommunity.com
PO Box 10082
Berkeley, CA 94709
Telephone: 800-260-5534
or 510-526-7106
info@livingtreecommunity.com
Living oils, raw nuts and nut
butters, olives, olive oil, agave
nectar, coconut butter, raw seeds,
and dried fruits and vegetables.

Maine Coast Sea Vegetables
www.seaveg.com
3 George's Pond Road
Franklin, ME 04634
Telephone: 207-565-2907
info@seaveg.com
Organic sea vegetables.

Mail Order Catalog
www.healthy-eating.com
413 Farm Road
PO Box 180
Summertown, TN 38483
Telephone: 800-695-2241
or 931-964-2241
Sprouting supplies and seeds, spiral
slicer, nutritional yeast, goji berries,
raw organic cacao nibs, raw organic
vegan cookies, sweets, and crackers.

Nature's First Law
(To order)
www.rawfood.com/cgi-
bin/order/index.cgi?af=1363
PO Box 900202
San Diego, CA 92190
Telephone: 800-205-2350
or 888-RAW-FOOD
nature@rawfood.com
Wild-crafted raw carob powder, raw
cashews, raw coconut butter, goji
berries, raw hempseeds and oil,
Himalayan salt, raw macadamia nuts,
Nama Shoyu, raw olives, Hunza
raisins, vanilla beans, Vita-Mix, spiral
slicer.

Visit the website:
http://www.aliveinfive.com

About the Author

*A*ngela *E*lliott is an Arizona native. She was raised by a world-renowned physicist/chemist stepfather and a gourmet French chef/writer mother whose occupations enabled frequent travel abroad and instilled in the young Angela a fascination with various cultures. Angela endeared herself to her lively Irish grandfather, a storyteller of some notoriety, and was encouraged to share her blossoming imagination with her peers. A passion for the arts was inspired by Angela's grandfather and mother, and instilled in her a lifelong love of literature and writing. Angela spent summers with her biological father, the head horticulturist for the San Diego Zoo, who sparked her interest in plants and the natural world.

A practitioner in holistic endeavors, including Chinese medicine, nutrition, herbology, reflexology, culinary arts, living food, and intuitive healing, Angela also has extensive experience as a licensed paramedical aesthetician. Angela has contributed to various publications, including *VegNews Magazine* and *Vegetarian Baby and Child Magazine*, and has taught gourmet classes, lectured, and on occasion toured with Lou Corona, a nationally recognized proponent of living food. She is the owner and operator of Celestial Raw Goddess Enterprises, which promotes raw food as a life-enhancing aspect of natural wellness.

Angela currently resides in San Diego, California, with her loving husband, Mike, her six-foot-three teenage son, Ian, and their two whacky but loveable Dalmatians, Molly and Bunker.

For television or radio bookings, interviews, lectures, or seminars with Angela Elliott, contact Celestial Raw Goddess Enterprises:

Telephone: 619-726-7685 E-mail: thegoddess@celestialrawgoddess.com

Index

A

agave nectar, raw, 12
almond butter, raw, in soup, 66
almond milk, 12, 18, 36, 43
  in desserts, 106, 108, 109, 120
  recipe for, 31
  in soups, 65, 66, 67
almond pulp, 12
  in appetizer, 43
  in breakfast recipes, 36, 37
  in sauce, 72
almonds, raw, 12
  in beverages, 28, 31
  in entrée, 100
apples, 20, 23
  in breakfast recipe, 36
  in dessert, 116–117
  in salad, 53
apricots, 20, 23
artichoke hearts, in entrée, 94–95
avocados, 20, 23
  in appetizers, 44, 45
  in breakfast recipe, 38
  in desserts, 104–105, 119
  in entrées, 82–83, 91, 96, 98,
    100, 101
  in salad, 60
  in soups, 62, 63, 67

B

bananas, 20, 23
  in beverages, 29, 33
  in dessert, 112
basil
  in entrées, 80–81, 86–87
  in sauces, 71, 76–77
  in soups, 64, 67
bell peppers
  in appetizers, 44, 46
  in entrées, 86–87, 88, 89, 96,
    98, 99
  in salad, 51
  in sauce, 78
  in soup, 65
berries, 23. *See also* specific types
  of
  in breakfast recipe, 37
black pepper, 12
blueberries, 20
  in breakfast recipe, 37
  in dessert, 118
  in salad, 50
bok choy, in entrée, 93
broccoli, in entrées, 90, 99
broccoli sprouts, in salad, 58

C

cabbage, in entrée, 98. *See also*
  other types of cabbage
cacao beans and nibs, raw, 12
  in desserts, 104–105, 109, 119,
    120
cantaloupes, 20, 23
carob powder, raw, 13
  in desserts, 104–105, 109, 119,
    120
carrots, 23
  in entrées, 97, 100
  grated, 19

  in salads, 53, 60
cashews, raw, 13
  in breakfast recipe, 37
  in dessert, 113
  in entrées, 92, 97
  in sauce, 72
cayenne, 13
  in entrées, 82–83, 88, 89, 90, 96
  in sauces, 74, 75, 76–77
  in soup, 63
celery
  in entrée, 84
  in salad, 53
  in soups, 62, 63, 66
cherries, 20, 23
  in desserts, 107, 121
cherry tomatoes, in salad, 59
chili powder, in entrées, 96, 96, 100
Chinese cabbage
  in entrée, 93
  in salad, 49
chives, in entrée, 91
cilantro
  in appetizers, 43, 45
  in entrées, 89, 96, 100
  in salad, 59
  in sauce, 71
  in soups, 63, 64, 65
cinnamon
  in breakfast recipe, 36
  in desserts, 109, 116–117, 118,
    120
clover sprouts
  in entrée, 98
  in salad, 58
coconut, dried
  in breakfast recipe, 39

in dessert, 106
in salad, 50
mangoes, 21, 24
in appetizer, 45
in beverage, 29
in dessert, 112
menu plans, 25–26
Mexican seasoning
in appetizer, 45
in entrées, 82–83, 89, 98
miso, unpasteurized, 14
in entrées, 82–83, 89
in sauce, 75
mung bean sprouts
in entrée, 97
in salad, 49
mushrooms
in appetizer, 46
in soup, 66

N

Nama Shoyu, 14
in entrées, 86–87, 93, 97, 99
in sauce, 75
in soup, 64
napa cabbage, in entrée, 97
Nature's First Law, 122
nectarines, 24
nori, raw, 15
in entrées, 84, 101
nut milk, straining, 18
nutritional yeast, 15
in appetizer, 43
in entrées, 80–81, 90, 94–95, 98
in sauces, 74, 75
nuts. *See also* specific types of
in appetizer, 43
in breakfast recipe, 37

in sauce, 72
soaking, 18

O

olive oil, 15
olives, 15
in appetizers, 42, 46
in entrées, 86–87, 94–95
in salad, 57
in sauces, 78
onions, in entrée, 98. *See also*
onions, red; onions, sweet
onions, red
in appetizer, 44
in salads, 51, 52
onions, sweet
in appetizers, 43, 45
in entrées, 84, 86–87, 91
in salad, 57
in sauce, 71
in soup, 63
oranges/orange juice, 21, 24
in beverages, 29, 33
in desserts, 112, 115
in entrée, 93
in sauce, 75
oregano, in soups, 64, 67

P

pantry staples, 12–16
papayas, 21, 24
parsley
in appetizer, 43
in entrée, 91
in soup, 66
passion fruit, 24
peaches, 21, 23

pears, 23
peas, in entrée, 99
pecan milk, 18, 39
in beverage, 120
in breakfast recipe, 39
in desserts, 106, 108, 109
recipe for, 34
pecan pulp, in breakfast recipe, 18, 39
pecans, raw
in beverage, 34
persimmons, 24
pineapples, 24
in beverage, 29
in dessert, 112
pine nuts, raw, 15
in entrée, 80–81
plums, 22, 24
probiotic powder, 15
in breakfast recipe, 37
in sauces, 70, 72
produce, 15, 23–24
pumpkin seeds, raw, 15

R

raisins, 15, 24
in breakfast recipe, 39
in salad, 53
raspberries, 22
romaine lettuce/romaine hearts, in
salads, 49, 57, 60, 82–83

S

sea vegetables, raw, 15
sesame oil, in entrée, 97
sesame seeds, raw, in entrée, 93
snow peas, in entrée, 93